Rhondda-Cynon-Taff County Borough Libraries
Llyfrgelloedd Bwrdeistref Sirol Rhondda-Cynon-Taf

School Library Service

If this book is found, please return it to the Schools Services Librarian, Mountain Ash Library.

Class _JF BLA_

No. _171735_

Julie Jones
County Borough Librarian

Autumn in the Dark Wood
Boy on a Hill Top
Christmas Cat
Christmas Present for a Friend
The Day I Got Better
Deep in the Dark Wood
Favourites
Firework Party
Holes
I Bet I Could
Jake
The Little Shepherd Boy
Martin the Cobbler
Oscar on the Moon
Rain
The Runaway Tram
The Smallest Christmas Tree
Snow in the Dark Wood
Spring in the Dark Wood
That Kind of Rabbit
The Tyre Dump

Blakeley, Peggy
   Favourites. — (Read together books)
I. Title II. Sugita, Yutaka III. Series
823'.914[J]   PZ7

ISBN 0-7136-2868-5

Published by A & C Black (Publishers) Limited
35 Bedford Row, London WC1R 4JH

This edition © 1986 A & C Black (Publishers) Ltd
First published 1979 by Shiko-Sha Co Ltd, Japan
under the title **Ureshiihi**
© original text and illustrations Yutaka Sugita

All rights reserved. No part of this publication may be reproduced,
stored in a retrieval system, or transmitted in any form or by any
means, electronic, mechanical, photocopying, recording or otherwise,
without the prior permission in writing of A & C Black (Publishers) Limited.

Filmset by August Filmsetting, Haydock, St Helens.
Printed in Japan

Favourites

Words by PEGGY BLAKELEY
Paintings by YUTAKA SUGITA

A & C BLACK · LONDON

I have lots of favourite things –
and some of them are balloons.
I like red ones best
and we had them at my birthday party.
It's great fun blowing them up
but it's a bit sad when they go 'pop!'

And I like my new welly boots.
I'd grown out of my others
so we had to go to town to buy these.
They're white
and they have yellow fur
that goes right down to the ends of the toes.
Now, when it rains, I can go 'slosh' through all the puddles.

One of my favourite things is digging.
I take Daddy's trowel from the shed
and go to my own bit of garden.
Daddy made it for me and I planted seeds there.
I get mucky – but it's fun.
And I do like to watch my flowers grow.

One of my best things is our bird.
He's called Charlie
and he lives in his cage in the window.
He chatters and sings
and sometimes he perches on my fingers
– if I keep very still.
When it's his bedtime, Mum covers him with a cloth.

I'm very proud of one of my favourite things.
One day, quite long ago, I planted
a little bulb in a pot.
We waited and waited
and now it's grown into a lovely flower.
Mum has put it on the sitting-room table
for everyone to see.

A very favourite thing of mine
is going for a walk to see Polly the pony.
She lives in a field near us
and when we go to see her, she comes trotting to the fence.
I think she knows I always bring some apples
for her.

And another of the things I like
is the blue chair at my granny's flat.
It has a yellow cushion
and is just the right size for me.
Granny says it belonged to her granny
when she was a little girl,
and it's very old and we must take care of it.
So we do.

Then there's the tree.
I do like it.
It's at the end of our garden, and on sunny days
we sit under it to have our elevenses.
And I climb it with the children next door.
Then, in the autumn, it turns all red and green.
It's magic.

One of my most favourite things is my
little sister. She's special.
She's only a baby, not a big girl like me
and I help her to drink her soup
from her own special cup.
She sits in her high chair
and chuckles fat chuckles at me.
And I laugh back.

Some of my best things are candles.
They make me think of Christmas
and birthdays.
They're lovely when they're lit
and then Daddy puts out our big lights
and the candles flicker in the darkness.
When it was my birthday I had 4 candles on my cake
– I blew them out in one go.

But my most favourite thing of all is my teddy.
I call him Bear and he goes everywhere with me.
Yesterday he came to the Teddybear's Picnic
at my school, and once he went with me
to a party at our library.
And now he's going to bed with me and
it's time to say
                Goodnight.

... and I also like my red umbrella
.... and my pink slippers
.... and Father Christmas
.... and ....

KS1-2
My favourite things
Things I like